A COMPLETE GUIDE TO RAISING MEAL WORMS

EVERYTHING YOU NEED TO KNOW TO RAISE YOUR OWN ENDLESS SUPPLY OF FREE MEAL WORMS

J. LYNN CURRIE

ACKNOWLEDGEMENTS

The author thanks his friend Jerry for introducing him to the meal worm and many fine times fishing together; his daughter, Jackie – a wonderful young lady who still goes fishing with her old man; his friend Jim for assistance in the mindset needed to undertake this effort; and, his wife, Susan, for her encouragement, support and cajoling in the completion of this guide (and use of her hand for the cover).

DEDICATION

To the memory of my son

Jason

who was the best son and camping/fishing/hunting companion.

Photographs and drawings by the author.
(Picture on Page 71 taken by Jason Currie.)

© Copyright 2007 by J. Lynn Currie

CONTENTS

INTRODUCTION 4

WHAT IS A MEAL WORM? 9

THE LIFE CYCLE OF A MEAL WORM 14

PREPARING THE MEAL WORM FARM 31

OBTAINING YOUR STOCK 39

QUICK START CHECKLIST 44

FEEDING YOUR MEAL WORMS 45

TENDING THE FARM 49

INCREASING THE HERD 57

FEEDING PETS MEAL WORMS 62

FISHING WITH MEAL WORMS 63

BIBLIOGRAPHY 73

INTRODUCTION

The sunshine sneaking between the clouds was just enough to make us comfortable in our tee shirts. It was a perfect spring day to hit the water and drown some worms with my friend Jerry.

Only, on this day I was fishing with worms that I'd never used before as bait. We both had a great time ... and caught fish.

That was about 35 years ago, but it changed my fishing fortunes ever since. These worms were such excellent bait that I had to ask about them.

To my surprise, they came out of a bucket in his utility room. He just grabs some when he goes fishing.

He told me that about all he does is give them a place to live and some trimmings of potatoes or carrots and such. I had him tell me everything he could about this because I wanted to raise my own.

My next stop at a bait shop included the purchase of meal worms. They are rather expensive by the dozen or so. But this time all of them weren't used as bait. Some of them became my first breeding stock for generations of meal worms to follow: meal worms that enhanced many a fishing trip by turning "fishing" in to "catching."

Meal worms serve many other purposes. One time, while tending to my meal worms, a fond thought came to mind. When I was grade school age I used to go to the Illinois state fair every year (the one in Springfield, IL). At that time many vendors were selling chameleons as pets. I talked my parents into buying one for me. I remembered that a favorite meal of my pet was a meal worm.

I have since learned that the meal worm serves as good, nutritious food for many animals that are kept as pets. These include exotic birds, mice, iguanas, frogs, turtles, rats, sugar gliders, and others. The meal worm is also used as wild bird food. They are supposedly well liked by blue birds. There are meal worm bird feeders available and at least one company sells roasted meal worms as bird food.

Meal worms are also used for educational purposes, primarily in the lower grades. They are used to teach about the life cycle of insects that undergo complete metamorphosis. Meal worms are used because they are easy to keep, they go through their life cycle within a school year, and they are readily examined by students. They have also been used over the years for varieties of entomological studies and research.

You may not want to hear this, but we can also eat them. Perhaps you have eaten chocolate covered ants or grasshoppers? Maybe not? One friend of mine says that he has actually eaten chocolate covered meal worms, but I've never seen one.

Many people have some aversion to eating "bugs." This distaste is not common throughout the world. Native Americans have and might eat various insects or arthropods such as spiders. Many insects are safe for human consumption, but not all of them.

The edible ones are high in protein. Some say that the meal worm is related to the mescal worm or the larval form of the moth Hypopta agavis, which you may have seen in a bottle of tequila or even a lollipop. Some meal worms may be used in tequila type candies. In South America you might find meal worms served with a dish of food and rice. I once ran across a recipe for a meal worm pizza. [I lost that one, but still have one for cicadas.]

Whatever your interest is in raising meal worms, I have written this so that you can do it. I am not an entomologist, but I have raised my own meal worms at home, several different homes, in different ways, places, and conditions for more than a quarter of a century.

My main reason for raising meal worms was to have a ready supply of free fish bait. There was also a time when it was handy to have some to supplement the diet of my son's iguana, Iggy.

Regardless of your reason, everything you need to know is included in this guide. The material here is based upon my years of experience, reading for my own knowledge, and research conducted in the preparation of this information for you. In this guide you will find all the basic information you need to know about meal worms: what they are; how they live; what and how to feed them; how to maintain their living space; how to keep them healthy; and, how to increase the number you have. For the fishermen and ladies I have also included some tips that may be helpful.

If you follow the instructions in this guide I guarantee that you will have your own supply of meal worms.

ADDITONAL INTRODUCTORY COMMENTS

There is always new information. I don't try to keep up with it since what I do, and am sharing with you, has worked for me. But you may have questions about the information in this guide. Because I want you to be successful, you may contact me through my website MEALWORMSFORFREE.COM.

Throughout this guide I refer to raising meal worms like farming. I call their containers "farms", the meal worms "stock", and a bunch of them a "herd". Hopefully you will appreciate that on a very small scale there are many similarities.

This is a guide to raising meal worms at home for the purposes of fish bait or pet food. You can easily raise hundreds or thousands, if you wish, using this information. However, this guide doesn't include everything there is to know about meal worms or raising them.

Different methods are used for different purposes. For example, if you were raising them in a classroom setting for educational purposes, there are things you might do differently. In that setting you might be satisfied with a smaller number of meal worms and set your meals worms up in an environment for maximum exposure to your students. Businesses that produce millions of meal worms for wholesale or for roasted bird food purposes use quite different methods.

There are a variety of species of insects that are related to what is referred to in this guide as meal worms. The ones that have been raised for bait or pet food are what you might call domesticated. They have been raised for many generations. You may find insects that look like meal worms in your trees or nuts of trees or compost that look like meal worms. Everything in this guide refers only to the meal worms that are typically sold as meal worms by bait shops or pet stores.

Finally, although I have not heard of it, there may be places where raising meal worms is illegal or has some legal restrictions. I can't, of course, assume any responsibility for such or any other matters related to how you use the information in this guide.

WHAT IS A MEAL WORM?

If you are reading this, you probably have a good answer to this question. The meal worm is the creature pictured on the front of this book, right? That is correct. However, what you see is a creature in one stage of its development. It looks completely different in other stages of its life.

In this picture, what we usually think of as the meal worm is shown with its adult counterpart.

The meal worm goes through several stages during its life cycle that are similar to, but different from, those of a butterfly. These things are explained in this guide.

A brief introduction to the meal worm is presented in this chapter. More detailed information about the meal worm and its life cycle are covered in the next chapter, THE LIFE CYCLE OF THE MEAL WORM. You may skip over that chapter at the moment if you are eager to get started. But do come back to it as it contains important information that will be useful to you. Besides, the meal worm isn't really a worm anyway.

IT ISN'T A WORM?

No, the meal worm isn't really a worm. What we usually call a meal worm is the larval form of an insect that looks sort of like a worm. It is generally between one half-inch to one inch long. The color varies from a yellowish light tan to a light brown. It has a head at one end of its body. There are six legs (part of the insect designation) on the under side of the body behind the head. The soft body is protected by a harder, segmented exoskeleton. And, a wonderful characteristic, if you are raising them, is that they can't climb up the sides of slick vertical surfaces.

The meal worm is also a nice little creature. The worm is comical in its clumsy crawling around. Although it feels funny, it will crawl around in your hand and it doesn't bite (that I know of).

The worm-like larvae of the insect may be called a meal worm for a number of reasons. They are referred to as both "meal worms" and also "mealworms", as in one word.

SO, WHY ARE THEY CALLED MEAL WORMS?

As far as I can tell, they are called worms just because they look like worms. And, "meal" worms because they make a tasty meal for other creatures. Not really, although that is true.

Part of their diet in the wild would include grains. As people grew grains agriculturally and stored them, their grain was sometimes infested with this wormy looking insect. These grains are often referred to as meal, especially when processed, like oat meal. Although I haven't seen it put this way, it is possible that upon finding these in their grains and meal, they became commonly called meal worms.

HOW DO MEAL WORMS REPRODUCE?

They don't. That is, the worms (larvae) don't reproduce. Over time a worm turns in to a pupa which then turns in to a beetle. The beetles mate and the female lays eggs which hatch in to little meal worms.

WHAT ELSE SHOULD I KNOW?

The most amazing thing to me is how easy they are to raise. Consider the following:

1. They take up very little space;

2. They mostly eat food scraps that you'd pitch or put in the compost;
3. They don't make any noise;
4. They can't escape their containers;
5. They breed readily and produce many offspring;
6. They don't create any obnoxious odors; and,
7. They require minimal attention and maintenance.

By little attention, I mean that when you follow the instructions in this guide you should be able to leave them unattended for a month or more. Minimal maintenance means that you should be able to let them be without any serious cleaning for six months to a year or more. When given a small amount of care they go about their business and reward you with many more meal worms.

WON'T THE BEETLES FLY AWAY?

You may have this concern about raising meal worms after seeing the picture of the beetle. You may be picturing beetles flying around your house like butterflies when they emerge from their cocoons.

That is understandable. When I moved what my wife calls my "pets" in to the house, she told me that if they start flying around, then both of us are in trouble.

Do not fret; I've not seen one fly yet. Nor has my friend. In terms of raising them, this is a good thing. It is obviously very good for many reasons.

The front wings of the beetle (elytra) lack veins and are not used for flight. The scientific name for the meal worm (the order), Cleoptera, is derived from Greek and means "sheath-winged". Basically, the wings are bound and useless for flight.

In all honesty, I have read one (and only one) account of meal worm beetles flying. The article didn't identify the specific genus or species. None the less, they would have to be something other than the ones that have been raised for fish bait or pet food.

If I was going to picture a flying meal worm, this is what I'd think of:

A FLYING MEAL WORM? ⟹ *Whee!*

THE LIFE CYCLE OF A MEAL WORM

This chapter presents more detailed information about the life cycle of the meal worm. You may not care about this at the moment or think it is very important. Yet, it is important to know about the stages in the life cycle so you aren't alarmed when your meal worms just lay there as if they're dying. Or, wonder why seemingly all of a sudden you have these alien looking things in your container. And so you won't be surprised to find your container full of beetles. You will understand that they are changing from one form in to another as part of their life cycle.

The meal worm looks different, acts different, and should be treated differently in each of its life stages. There are aspects to each stage which are also useful to know for improving your ability to successfully raise meal worms.

WHAT IS THE BASIC LIFE CYCLE?

As mentioned before, the meal worm is actually the larval form of an insect. Although there are many species, the most common is referred to as Tenebrio molitar, or T. molitar. You may also see references to subspecies such as Tenebrio molitar L.

The scientific classification for an insect generally called a meal worm is shown below.

Animalia	(kingdom)
Arthropoda	(phylum)
Insecta	(class)
Coleoptra	(order)
Tenebrionidae	(family)
Tenebrio	(genus)
Molitar	(species)

These insects have a life cycle similar to butterflies. A butterfly starts out as an egg, hatches as a larva (the caterpillar), changes in to a pupa (inside the cocoon), and finally emerges as a butterfly. This process is called complete metamorphosis.

The meal worm also undergoes complete metamorphosis; though in a slightly different manner. It starts as an egg. When the egg hatches, out comes the larva (the form we call the meal worm). The meal worm grows until it changes in to a pupa – without the cocoon. The life cycle may remind you of something you've seen before (perhaps in a school science or biology class?), as represented by the diagram on the next page.

EGG   LARVA

(Meal Worm)

This diagram portrays the stages in the life cycle of the meal worm.

The four stages represent the undergoing of complete metamorphosis.

BEETLE   PUPA

The remainder of this chapter discusses each stage of the meal worm life cycle. Each section contains a description of the appearance of the meal worm in each stage, length of the stage, and related information. You will notice that the length of time the meal worm may be in each stage varies greatly. Although I have a general idea of how long my meal worms spend in each stage, I have had no need to keep track of this information. The time frames given have been taken from sources listed in the bibliography.

HOW ABOUT THE MEAL WORM ITSELF?

Which came first, the beetle or the egg? Probably neither ... at least in terms of raising them. You will probably start as I did with the meal worm itself. Hence this journey through the life cycle begins with the larval form of the meal worm. After all, the larvae we use as bait or pet food are the most important part to us and those with which we likely start our meal worm farms. Some mature larvae, that we call meal worms are pictured below.

In essence, the meal worm begins its life as a very small larva hatching out of an egg. You probably need a microscope or at least a strong magnifying glass to see one. I rarely notice one until it is visible to the naked eye crawling around in a container.

The primary mission of larvae is to eat and grow. They do not have bones, but an exoskeleton. The exoskeleton is segmented in to a number of rings surrounding the body. The segments are linked together in a way that gives them some flexibility while still maintaining protection. But once fully established the exoskeleton doesn't grow. In this sense, meal worms are sort of like snakes. That is, they have to shed their exoskeleton and grow another one.

When the meal worm begins to outgrow its exoskeleton, it molts. The outgrown exoskeleton is shed and a new one is grown. The period between each molting is called an instar. It will go through 10 to 20 instars before it is fully grown.

After each molting the meal worm is lighter in color. During the instar period the new exoskeleton hardens and darkens to the shiny, honey-golden color that contributes to some people calling it a golden grub. Then it molts again and again until it is mature and ready to morph in to a pupa.

The following illustration points out the major parts of the meal worm. The meal worm lives in this form, eating and growing through instars, while a larva.

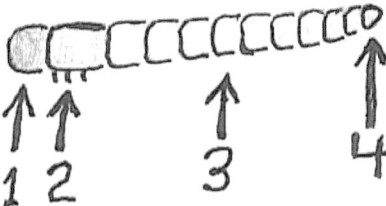

This drawing points out the four main parts of the meal worm. These are described below.

1. This is the head. It is the semi-circular and darker part at the larger end of the meal worm. This is usually the darkest part of the meal worm. If you examine the meal worm closely you will see that it has a mouth and eyes.
2. Behind the head is the largest segmented section of the meal worm. This segment connects the head to the rest of the body and serves as the body part that supports the legs. This part is usually somewhat less dark than the head.
3. The rest of the body consists of additional segments that contain the digestive tract. These are usually the lighter parts of the meal worm.
4. This is the tail end of the meal worm. The meal worm narrows from head to tail and tends to get slightly darker in color towards the end. Waste is eliminated at the tail end of the meal worm.

At some point in time you will notice that it looks like your meal worms are dying. They will become inactive and just lay there or roll over. Unless you have a serious problem with your meal worms, they are not dying. They are beginning to morph in to the next stage of their life cycle.

In my years of raising meal worms I have never had a problem that wiped out one of my farms. By following the basic instructions about caring for your meal worms in this guide you shouldn't have any problems either. From things I've read it is possible for your herd to become infected with some kind of viral or bacterial diseases, but this is unlikely as long as you do the basics to keep your meal worms healthy.

I should have known better, but one time a couple of years ago I thought I was losing my meal worms. Then I realized that some moth balls had been moved in to the small storage room where the farms were. (I think I did it without thinking.)

Since moth balls are not so good for many insects (and even us people), I thought that maybe I had inadvertently killed my meal worms. I was concerned because I had many generations of meal worms with new stock that had been added off and on over the years. As a result, my stock tends to begin morphing at various times, not usually all at once. This time the whole herd was taking on the appearance of dying meal worms.

Well, I moved [and sealed] the moth balls and let the meal worms be. I was glad to see that within a couple of days that they were alive and morphing in to pupae.

The first time you see your meal worms beginning the process of morphing in to pupae might be alarming. Be patient and enjoy the awesome transformation taking place in front of your eyes.

How long do your meal worms live as meal worms? Based on things I've read, they exist as larvae for either 3 months, 10 weeks, or 30 to 90 days in warm weather. So, your meal worms are larvae for some where between one and three months.

The next section gives you basic information about the pupae. This is the stage of the life cycle between the larvae and the beetles.

WHAT IS THE PUPA?

When your meal worms begin to pupate and morph in to pupae they will appear to be dead for a couple of days or so. Be patient because this process can take a little time. The final exoskeleton is shed and the meal worm takes on a completely different appearance. One day the meal worm looks like it is dead. The next day it looks like an alien being.

This is the beginning of a delicate time in the life cycle. The meal worms only look dead but they are very much alive. Unless you want to use them for a specific purpose they should not be bothered while they pupate. In the following picture you can identify mature larvae, shed exoskeleton, and newly morphed pupae. No wonder they use meal worms in science classes; the change is like science fiction.

The pupae may also seem to be dead but they are very busy. They mostly just lay there. They do not eat. For all practical purposes they have no mouth or legs. Yet, moment by moment they are developing.

A closer look at a pupa shows the miraculous transformation from a meal worm. A newly morphed pupa will be slightly off-white/very pale yellow in color and slightly bent. The form of the meal worm is almost completely lost.

While it is a pupa the meal worm undergoes changes similar to those of a butterfly pupa under cloak of a cocoon. Without this covering protection, you could say that it is naked at this time. This is why it is especially vulnerable. The benefit, primarily for educational purposes, is that the change takes place in full sight.

 As the pupa develops it starts to look more and more like a beetle. The primary job of the pupa is to morph in to its adult form, the beetle. Its activity is mostly internal, and manifested externally. It is passive, yet if you touch it, it will wiggle. Touch pupae gently if you must.

How long do they stay in this stage? As mentioned the possible time frames are quite broad. This is also true for the pupae. The ranges mentioned by authors on the subject vary from 6 or 7 to 10 or 30 days; 10 to 20 days; or up to 3 weeks. So, your pupae will be such somewhere between about one to three weeks before they morph into the adult form of the meal worm – the beetles.

WHAT ABOUT THE BEETLES?

Once a pupa is close to becoming a young adult, as in the picture on the next page, it will become a beetle quickly. The pupa ecloses in to an adult. The young beetle is a light brownish/dark gray color. Within days it will turn dark brown to black. With some meal worms the beetle is commonly called a Darkling Beetle.

After the pupa becomes an immature eclosed beetle it will mature in a couple of days to a week or so. At this point it will not grow much. It will eat and mature. Its primary purpose is to mature and mate.

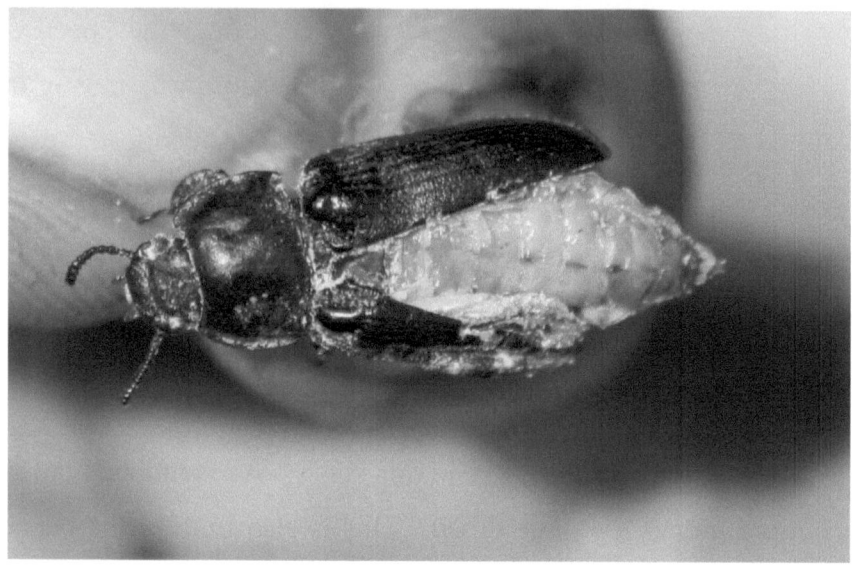

This is a pupa morphing in to a beetle. It already has its beetle head and partially developed legs on the underside. The wings and the rest of the body are still in transition.

Your meal worms, at least in the beetle stage, are males and females. If you start with one or two dozen larvae you should have enough beetles of both sexes. Treat them right and keep them happy and your females will reward you with plenty of eggs.

It appears that the females will lay their eggs wherever they want. It is generally stated that they lay eggs in the bedding. I believe that they pick some spot which is instinctually chosen to be a place that is viable for survival of the eggs. This may be any good spot in your container.

I think they may also lay eggs in holes in potatoes or such that were eaten previously by larvae or maybe even beetles. My thoughts on this are explained in other parts of this guide. As with the pupae, I also suggest leaving the beetles alone as much as possible. They are your breeding stock. If you have no beetles laying eggs, then you will have no more meal worms.

The beetles are also fragile in their own way, especially when immature. Even when they are mature, if you tip them over they may lay there thrashing like a turtle on its back. So I try to leave them alone as much as possible.

After the beetles have grown and bred, they die. Don't worry about some dead beetles in your meal worm containers to start with. Some of the carcasses will likely be eaten by other meal worms.

How long do they remain beetles? According to things I've read: they live 5 to 10 days; die after a couple of weeks; live around 4 weeks; or, live about 3 months. It depends on a number of factors. In a setting averaging around 66 degrees it is my experience that they may be around for longer than 3 months.

This is the underside of a mature beetle.

HOW ABOUT THE EGGS, THEN?

As you may gather from the above discussion, the female is likely to lay her eggs here or there as she pleases. Like all eggs, the embryo develops until it hatches. Evidently no body knows much more than this about the meal worm egg.

I have not seen a meal worm egg. I haven't seen a picture of a meal worm egg. Surely they are very small and my camera isn't up to that. I just know they are there because I get more meal worms!

Depending on what you read, a female beetle will lay between 70 to 100 eggs, or between 275 and 500 eggs. Some body had to see them to count them? It is not that important for raising them. If you have several female beetles that lay several hundred eggs ... you get my point.

How long are meal worms in the egg stage? Well, from what I have read it could be 4 to 11 days or it could be from 7 days up to 4 weeks.

FINAL COMMENTS ON THE LIFE CYCLE

Hopefully you can see how important it is to understand the basics of the meal worm life cycle. Throughout this guide I will refer to the life cycle as it relates to various aspects of raising them.

If you follow all of the suggestions in this guide you will likely have times when your farm has meal worms in all stages of development. The picture on the next page is looking down in to a small "plastic" hotel trash container (about 9 X 6" internal dimensions). You should be able to identify meal worms as larvae, pupae, and beetles. The larvae are both on top and below the bedding. The pupae are found mostly on top of the bedding. Beetles are mostly on top of the bedding, but they do burrow and will do so to hide when you disturb them.

In this picture you will see two beetles on what you may recognize as a small piece of bread. There is also a dark looking something which is the dried outside of a piece of apple and some pieces of drying potato. These things are explained later.

Can you see the larvae, pupae, and beetles? This is an actual picture of one of my small farms in which the meal worms were in each of these stages simultaneously.

Outside of the fact that the length of time a meal worm is any stage of development may vary greatly, there are other factors that may explain why you have meal worms in all stages at one time. Some of these factors are the ways you maintain the health of your herd or increase the size of your herd.

The next two pages present a summary of the life cycle time frames. For the most part, the length of time your meal worms will spend in each cycle will depend upon the temperature, humidity, feeding, crowding, and their general health.

THE LENGTH OF LIFE CYCLE CHART

The chart on the next page starts with the egg stage of the meal worm and progresses through the adult beetle stage. The differences in the possible length of time in each stage is truly amazing.

This chart is based on published information about the subject. The time frames are all in weeks. The length that is labeled short is based upon the shortest time frames in the literature. The time frames that are labeled long are based upon the longest time frames I've seen in the literature.

According to this information, your meal worms could complete their life cycle in as little as seven weeks. Or, they could take as much as thirty-three weeks (more than half a year) to go through their life cycle. My guess is that your meal worms will go through their life cycle somewhere in the middle of this range. This is only provided for your information.

Just remember, these are the four stages your meal worms will go through. Be patient and know how to make the best of each stage.

The next chapter explains how to set up your meal worm farm. It is a good thing to do before you obtain your initial stock.

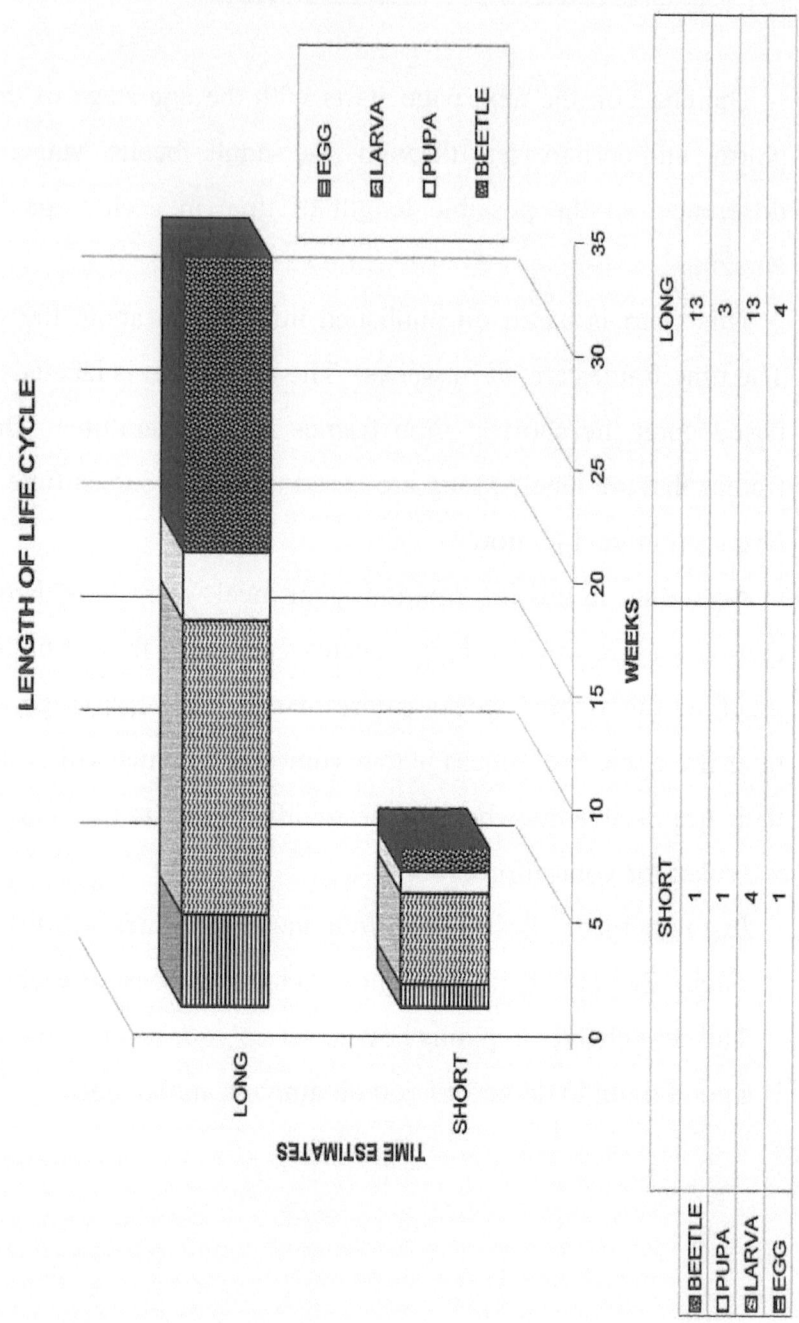

PREPARING THE MEAL WORM FARM

By analogy, meal worms are your livestock. Many are your herd. Where they live is your meal worm farm.

In other words, the farm is where you keep them. This chapter explains how to select a container, where to put it, and how to set it up to receive your initial stock.

WHAT KIND OF CONTAINER DO I USE?

Before you even obtain your initial stock it is a good idea to decide what kind and how large a container you want to start with for your farm. This will partly depend on where you want to keep the farm and how many you want to start to raise. Read through this chapter before you decide.

Basically almost anything with slick, smooth sides that are vertical or nearly straight up and down can be used to keep meal

worms. At different times I have used a variety of containers. (The one on the right is the one containing the farm pictured previously.)

A five gallon plastic pail, as shown, is excellent for the purpose. I have used them as well as dish tubs, kitty litter boxes, and small plastic trash cans. A plastic shoe or sweater box may even serve your purposes. Aquariums are most frequently used in classroom settings. If you have one that leaks, and it is only a small crack (which you fill even though it doesn't have to be waterproof), you could put it to this use. As I write this I have some in a 5 pound coffee can. You undoubtedly have something around that will work for starters.

Whatever kind of container you use, make sure it is clean before setting it up. This is especially true if you use a container that held chemicals or was used as a cleaning bucket. You want to rid the container of chemical residues. So, don't even bother using anything that contained pesticides.

WHERE DO I KEEP THE MEAL WORMS?

You can keep your meal worms most anyplace where it doesn't freeze and doesn't stay over 80 degrees Fahrenheit with high humidity. Some would suggest that a range of 45 to 85 degrees is acceptable, with an ideal temperature being around 77 degrees. Others note that in the wild they prefer dark, moist places with temperatures of 80 to 90 degrees. I believe that they adapt to a variety of conditions. However, those conditions likely affect the time it takes the meal worm to progress through its life cycle.

I have kept them in a basement where the winter temperature would fall to under 60 and the summer temperature would exceed

80 degrees Fahrenheit. I've also kept them in a spare room where the summer temperature would sometimes exceed 85 before I turned on the A/C. At the time of this writing I have some on a shelf in a storage room in the basement. This is a good location as they are out of the way, the temperature ranges from around 65 to 75 degrees, and there are two small windows that provide adequate indirect day light.

Although meal worms may mostly be found in dark and moist places in the wild, I recommend against raising them in total darkness or damp conditions. They can obviously tolerate light, as evidenced by their use in classrooms. I read in one source that some light everyday is beneficial. Yet, I'd also suggest against a location with lengthy direct sun light. This is to avoid overheating of the meal worms or their bedding. In my experience a combination of high temperature and high humidity has a tendency to do what I can only describe as melting my meal worms. Excessive humidity can also contribute to the development of mold in your meal worm farm.

In deciding where to locate your container, there are a few other important considerations to keep in mind. I recommend that you pay attention to the suggestions listed below.

1. Don't put the container over or next to an oven or close to ventilation ducts.
2. Don't place the container where the meal worms would be subject to drafts of hot or cold air such as opening doors in the heat of summer or freezing winter.

3. Don't place your meal worms where someone, including pets, might knock them over. They are safe in the container, but if they're on the floor they will crawl all over.
4. Avoid locations where anything might fall in to the container allowing the meal worms to escape. For example, curtains blowing in to the farm. They can't climb up the side of your container, but they can and will climb out on curtains. [I know this from personal experience!]
5. Keep your meal worms out of areas where other critters such as mice, raccoons, or opossums could get at them.
6. Try to avoid placing your container in a location where there are other insects that might move in with your meal worms.

Once you've decided where to place your meal worm farm you can choose the kind and size of container to set up as your farm. If you want to start with a large number of meal worms and raise many hundreds, you will probably want to start with something the size of the five gallon bucket. Otherwise, any of the smaller kind of containers should serve your purpose.

WHAT DO I DO WITH THE CONTAINER NOW?

Now that you've decided on a container and picked a place to put it, it's time to set up house. It is time to complete preparations for your meal worms. There are only two things to do in order to ready your farm for your first meal worm live stock.

The first thing is to provide bedding for your stock. Your domestically raised meal worms need bedding to live on, in, and usually eat. The only thing this means is putting an inch or so of certain grain or grain bran in the bottom of the container.

Wheat bran is considered excellent bedding. Oat bran is also good. I don't know what it is, but if you have it ... chicken mash is recommended by some. It may not represent best practice, but I usually use a lot of oatmeal (the natural whole grain kind that you might have for breakfast) mixed with some corn meal, and throw in a little bit of oat or wheat bran depending on what's handy.

The exact mixture isn't critical. The oatmeal provides good bedding and I believe it absorbs excess moisture. I use four to six or more times as much oatmeal as corn meal to start a container because corn meal is added off and on as food. The wheat or oat bran I add is a small amount, like a tablespoon or so; but this is not necessary to get started. The amounts you use will vary with the size of your container.

The second thing is to provide a source of moisture. Depending on the size of your container, add one or two small slices of potato. This is what almost everyone recommends as a way to make moisture available. Supposedly they drink from it. I have always thought that they eat it. But either way, it is a good thing. If you don't have any potato on hand you can use a small piece of carrot or apple. By small I mean about a quarter inch of potato or apple or one inch of a medium sized carrot halved, using both halves. Whatever you use, wash it first.

The next picture is a large one but I hope it helps you see how a meal worm farm might be set up. It may also give you some other ideas as to possible containers for your farm.

The container pictured is about a 2 ½ to 3 gallon glass crock. It is made of thick glass and is heavy. It shows an adequate depth of oatmeal and corm meal bedding for starting a small farm, along with the potato slice.

In the past I have only used this crock as a small aquarium with an under gravel filter. I set it up as a meal worm farm for the purposes of a picture for this guide. However, now since it is set up I will use it for that purpose. It came with a lid that I can put on for decorative purposes (as long as there is air flow). And then I can keep a closer eye on my meal worms or use it as a conversation piece in my study.

The point is that you have a large choice of things you can use as containers. They can be whatever is handy, whatever is practical, or something more aesthetic. While cleaning a farm recently I used the crock part of a crock pot that quit working years ago as a temporary holding pen for one of my farms.

The container you see above is about nine inches in diameter on the inside. The bedding consists of close to half of an 18 ounce box of oats, one-fourth cup of corn meal, and the potato slice. The corn meal was poured on top of the oatmeal. It works its way in to the oatmeal because of its smaller size. Believe it or not, there are also a couple of beetles, larvae, and tiny to middle size meal worms in there. Doesn't seem like much, but it will become a thriving farm. Those few meal worms in this container came from my stock. When you start you will have to get your initial stock to get your farm going. The next chapter discusses getting this done.

OBTAINING YOUR STOCK

Assuming you have no meal worms, you will have to get some meal worms (or beetles or pupae) to start your meal worm farm. Technically you could also start with eggs, but I have never heard of those being available. The easiest way to get started is by obtaining some meal worms (the larvae). And this is easily enough done.

There are many ways you can obtain your initial starter culture (or stock) of meal worms. In most or many parts of the country they can be purchased at a local fishing bait shop. They are sold at many pet shops. And, you can purchase them over the internet. I recommend the local bait shop.

WHY SHOULD I BUY THEM FROM A BAIT STORE?

If you go fishing, one of the places where you buy bait probably sells meal worms. Around these parts they are sold in little plastic containers of two to three dozen. That is a good amount to start your farm.

I recommend the bait shop because it is easy and convenient. And, unless you want to buy a thousand the price is probably cheapest at a bait store. The prices can vary widely; still you ought to be able to get your starters for under $3. In 2005 I bought 3 dozen for $1.35. Yes, that is dated information. I don't have much need to buy them. If I remember correctly mine were mostly in the pupae, beetle, and maybe egg stage at that time and I didn't want to bother them to pick out the larvae that were there. Although it is possible that I just forgot to harvest some. Those are the only two reasons that I buy meal worms any more.

As a cautionary comment, you may not want to buy the really large ones that are referred to as "giant" meal worms for breeding purposes. These are good fishing bait, but they may be less good for breeding stock. In the past I never bought them because of the price, going around $1.99 for 35. Though, that's not a bad price for buying good live bait?

From what I've read, they are "giant" meal worms because they may have been treated with an insect growth hormone that delays morphing. Hence, they grow bigger. One statement I read expressed doubts about the ability of these meal worms to reproduce. In terms of raising them, you want them to morph naturally and become breeding adults.

I was introduced to some of these giant meal worms on a fishing trip with my friend Don. He let me take the ones that survived the fishing trip home with me. There weren't very many so I added them to one of my containers.

Within two weeks they started to morph. Whether they reproduced is questionable as following generations of meal worms weren't giants. But without the growth hormone their progeny may have been the usual size.

I would avoid using these as your starter stock. Why bother? I just cannot predict your results. You can always experiment later if that's something you would like to try.

WHAT ABOUT THE FISH OR PET STORE?

If you visit a tropical fish store you may be able to purchase meal worms there. This is more likely if the business also sells other exotic pets. The cost will likely be a little higher than at the bait shop.

A pet store that sells iguanas, horned toads, and any of the other pets that eat meal worms as part of their diet will probably have meal worms available for purchase. Again, the cost will more than likely be higher than what you'd pay at a bait shop.

CAN I BUY THEM OVER THE INTERNET?

Yes, you can also purchase meal worms over the internet. However, with the businesses I've found selling them, you often have to buy a whole lot of them or pay a whole lot for them.

As an example of what is available over the internet, I am listing some sites that sell meal worms. Some are next day delivery with no additional costs. Some sites are primarily for businesses that sell a wide variety of products. Those meal worms are priced at a little over $8 to about $16 per thousand. Those are good prices for a thousand, if you want that many.

The following were active sites at the time of writing. If you are interesting in making an online purchase, you should do your own search and find what is best for you.

www.superwormfarm.com
www.flukerfarms.com
www.expresscrickets.com
www.ReptileFood.com
www.SongbirdGarden.com
www.nottawildbirdsupply.com
www.Ghann.com
www.wormman.com
www.nyworms.com

As mentioned elsewhere, meal worms are also used in schools for educational purposes. You can purchase meal worms through companies that specialize in providing educational materials to schools and teachers. As an example, I found the site below which sells meal worms in the larval stage, as adults, or a combination of both. The prices range from about $6.50 to $9 depending on what you order.

http://wardsci.com

NOW WHAT DO I DO WITH THEM?

It doesn't matter how you obtain your starter stock of meal worms. Once you have them, you are ready to go. Your meal worms will come in some kind of bedding. Simply empty the meal worms and bedding (gently) in to your farm.

Now you are a meal worm farmer! The next page is a quick start checklist to remind you of what to do to get to this point. The following two chapters give information on how to feed and take care of your meal worms.

QUICK START CHECK LIST

This is a summary of the steps necessary to set up your meal worm farm. Refer to the relevant sections for detailed information.

___ **DECIDE ON A LOCATION**

    ___ The location is not too hold, cold, or humid; and not subject to extreme, rapid changes in temperature.
    ___ The location is safe from being knocked over and from having things fall in to it.
    ___ The location is safe from animals and other pests.

___ **PICK YOUR CONTAINER**

    ___ The container has smooth, slick, vertical sides.
    ___ The container is clean.

___ **SET UP THE FARM**

    ___ Put your bedding in the container.
    ___ Add a slice of potato (or carrot) to the bedding.

___ **INTRODUCE YOUR STOCK**

    ___ Obtain your meal worms and gently add them to the farm.

FEEDING YOUR MEAL WORMS

Meal worms in the wild are considered scavengers. They live in and around rotting wood. They also live in ant or termite hills. They eat decaying organic matter, including other dead insects. I believe the larvae will eat dead meal worm beetles.

SO WHAT DO I FEED THEM?

The main items on the menu for your meal worms will be grains. For the most part, they will eat the grains you supply as bedding.

Over time you will notice the bedding becoming finer, and finer. This is the result of it being eaten. The finer, almost dust size, particles are small pieces of grain and meal worm excrement. I won't venture to say that it's clean, but as long as the farm is tended to halfway decently there is no noticeable odor.

As the grains in the bedding are eaten more should be added. I can give little guidance in terms of how much because that depends on how many meal worms you have and how much you otherwise supplement their diet. One way to get an idea of how much and how fast they are eating is to put a small amount like a tablespoon of grain in one pile and then see how long it takes for it to disappear.

A sprinkling of additional corn meal or bran over the top of the bedding is a good way to add bedding and food. Don't be afraid of sprinkling grain over the meal worms. They burrow through grains anyway. I don't, however, suggest burying them either. The beetles are a slightly different story. They are less agile. When I have many beetles I add grain in piles at corners away from the beetles or along the edges of the container. The same goes for the pupae, which should be left alone as much as possible.

Supper is served.

If you are going away for an extended period of time your meal worms should do fine with a little extra food. Add a fresh slice of potato before you leave. You may want to leave two slices or a bigger piece than usual. Give them some fresh corn meal or other grain. And, of course, check on them upon your return.

WHAT ELSE DO THEY EAT?

Meal worms will eat many things. Just remember, they are <u>meal</u> worms. They do fine with adequate grains and something for moisture.

I think the potato is the main thing used for moisture because it holds moisture for a longer period of time. If your potato is dried up or perchance starting to rot or mold, replace it. The same is true for any foods. The bedding and grains should never become moldy. If for some reason that happens, follow the instructions for cleaning your containers set forth in the next chapter.

Unless you already have a fresh slice of potato or some other moisture food in your container you can always add some peelings from carrots or apples. On occasion I have given mine a bit of broccoli and cauliflower stalk, and even very small pieces of watermelon rind. I tried cabbage once, but I think it gave them gas!? Maybe not, but they didn't seem to care for it very much. You can also give them a small piece of natural type whole wheat or multi-grain bread. I say small because a large piece may get moldy before it is eaten, depending on the size of your herd.

ANYTHING ELSE I NEED TO KNOW?

Well, as you can tell the amounts of whatever you feed your meal worms varies upon how many you have in a container, the temperature and humidity, how much they eat, and the kinds of things you feed them. The main thing is to feed them well without over doing it. I don't have, nor have I seen a formula, for doing this. The intricacies of this process are left to your experience.

In general you can't overdo it with adding grains. You will have to get a feel for the moisture providing feed and anything else you decide to try. If you want to try something, I offer this suggestion. Take a very small portion and place it in a corner or against the side of your container. Take a look at it the next morning or evening and see if your meal worms are eating it. If they are, it will be partially gone or else you will see them all over it. If it is still there unbothered, it probably isn't good meal worm food. Take it out.

In my experience the beetles will pay more attention to the moisture food than the larvae. And, the pupae do not eat.

One final comment in regard to feeding: wash off the potato, carrots, apples, and such. You don't want to inadvertently introduce pesticides in to your meal worm farm.

This is something you don't need to know, but it is interesting. Your meal worms aren't completely quiet.

Noisy meal worms? I have never counted but I have read that the meal worm has three sets of jaws to help it eat. It must be true. I say that because one thing I know is that when they are busy eating (which is most of the time), you can put your ear down over their container and actually hear them eating. It is a bit eerie. Give a listen once you have a good sized herd.

TENDING THE FARM

Yes, your meal worm farm requires minimal attention and maintenance, but it does require some. Fortunately it doesn't take much as long as you don't over do the moisture foods, keep an eye on them, and don't have seriously over crowded conditions. This chapter tells you how to take care of your meal worms on a regular basis and ways to take care of a major cleaning which you may have to do every year or two.

HOW DO I KEEP MY MEAL WORM FARM CLEAN?

The only regular cleaning you have any need to be concerned about has to do with the pieces of moisture food and anything other than grains that you may feed your meal worms. Always remove anything that begins to rot or mold. I also suggest removing any pieces of carrot, apple, and non-grain foods that have dried up. You will notice that your meal worms will tend to leave them alone after they reach this condition.

There is one exception to the removal of large drying potatoes. I purposefully put pieces of potato that are about one-quarter of a small to medium size potato in the farm when beetles are present. Unless the pieces become rotten or moldy I leave them until some time after the beetles have died. My reason for this is explained in the next chapter.

WHAT MAJOR CLEANING DO I NEED TO DO?

Unless you have a very large number of meal worms for the size of your container you are unlikely to need to clean the container more than once every year or two. In this section I explain how to know when your farm needs cleaning. I also recommend cleaning the container if it becomes over crowded and either moving the meal worms to a bigger container, starting a second container, or taking some fishing. And, of course, you can clean up your farm any time you feel like it.

As you now know, some time after the beetles mate and lay eggs they die. Your container will have dead beetles in it. Unless it bothers you it doesn't matter. You can let the dead beetle carcasses stay until such time that you do a major cleaning.

WHEN DO I NEED TO CLEAN THE FARM?

You remember that the primary job of the meal worm is to eat and grow until it morphs in to a pupa. Needless to say, with all that eating there is a fair amount of excrement produced. Over time you will notice that the bedding slowly turns into more of a powder. This is mostly a result of the meal worms digesting the grains and other foods. If your container is not eventually cleaned your meal worms will end up living in their own excrement. This is not healthy. So, when a lot, or a majority, of your bedding consists of these powdery substances it is time to undertake a major cleaning.

The picture below shows the contrast between fresh and well used bedding. The old bedding pictured started out like the fresh bedding on the left. Over time it also had potato, carrot, more grains, and maybe a piece of bread added. You can see that the oatmeal has been pulverized. Corn meal is fine to start with, but it also becomes finer with small dark pieces. And, if you use yellow corn meal it will become more pale and gray in color.

It is nice to be able to harvest a couple dozen meal worms whenever you like. Still, it is possible for your farm to become too crowded. There are probably some guidelines having to do with optimum number of meal worms per cubic foot or something, but I don't know of any. Besides, who wants to count them? I tried once and it was a pain.

Usually a smaller container will become crowded sooner than a larger container. It also will depend upon the number with which you start and the many other conditions mentioned in this guide. Regardless of the size of the container, here is a simple way to judge if your meal worms are too crowded. If the surface is covered with meal worms to the extent that they have virtually no room to move without crawling over each other, they are too crowded. I'd say that they were too crowded a bit before they reached that point. Your herd will be healthier and stay cleaner if they are not over crowded. Remember that in addition to the meal worms you see on the surface, there are more of them (probably the majority of them) in the bedding.

HOW DO I CLEAN THE FARM?

The best time to clean a container is when all of the meal worms are worms – in the larval stage. This isn't always possible. I often have larvae, pupae, and beetles at the same time in one container. At such times I suggest waiting until the pupae have fully morphed into beetles.

The easiest way to clean a container is to set up another container and transfer the meal worms to a clean farm. This is also the best way to avoid throwing out the babies with the bath water, so to speak. By that I mean that there may be meal worms in your bedding that you can't see or eggs that haven't hatched that you don't want to pitch with the old bedding.

To do this, simply set up another container like you did to start your first meal worm farm. Catch your meal worms and move them to their new home. Then you can dispose of the old bedding and clean the container, keeping it for the next cleaning.

There are a number of ways to catch the meal worms. One way is to literally catch them. Pick them up in your hands and move them. If you already have more meal worms than you need, this method will suffice.

Doing it this way, by hand, has its drawbacks. You are likely to move more of the old bedding in to the new farm than you'd like. It is difficult to catch the baby meal worms. And, it is easy to injure the meal worms in the process. It is good to avoid injuring the meal worms so they don't become vulnerable to infection. Also, if there are eggs in the bedding, you may leave part of a soon to be generation behind.

The following is the method I use to move meal worms from one container to another. Basically, I catch them by "trapping" them over a couple of days. And I forgo cleaning the old farm for up to a month. This process allows you to leave pupae alone for the most part. You are also giving eggs time to hatch and baby meal worms enough time to grow to be noticeable.

I use part of a paper plate as my trap. Depending on the size of the plate and the container, the plate is cut so that the part used covers about one-fourth of the surface area.

That part of the plate is placed gently on the surface in a corner, against a side, or at the end of the container. If there are pupae or beetles in the area, you can use a spoon or such to gently move them out of the way.

If you have fresh bits of any moisture food in the container, remove them. Place some small fresh pieces of potato, carrot, or apple on the plate. Within an hour or so you should have meal worms on the plate. Pick up the plate and carefully let them slide in to their new home, along with any beetles that may be there. Replace the plate with food and check it later, repeating the process.

Do this a couple of times a day for a couple of days and you should have successfully moved most of your herd.

You now have two containers. Check the old farm off and on. If you left pupae in there, scoop them up after they've fully morphed in to beetles and move them in to the new farm. Look for meal worms and if you see any trap them the same way and move them as well. You can check the old farm every few days and repeat the process for a month or so, until there appears to be no more meal worms in the container, or until you get tired of it.

When you are ready to clean the container, dispose of the old bedding in your garden or compost. Then wash the container with some regular dish soap, hot water, and elbow grease. Avoid using harsh chemicals. You can use bleach, but rinse well. If you are keeping your meal worms in an aquarium, you should adhere to standard aquarium cleaning practice.

That completes the cleaning process! You ought to be another year or two older before you do that again. Isn't that a good thing?

But maybe you don't mind tending to two meal worm farms, or you want more so that you can have an even bigger herd? If so, the next chapter is for you.

ADDITIONAL TIPS ON CARING FOR YOUR FARM

Before you move on to the next chapter there are a couple of things you should keep in mind. They may never relate to your situation but they are useful to know.

The first thing has to do with spiders. They are great outside where they belong. Yet, it seems that they always find a way into the house. If you find spider webs in or around your farm I suggest that you remove them. I have never seen one of my meal worms in a spider web but I have no reason to think that a spider wouldn't have at one.

The second thing has to do with fruit flies and such. These little flying pests also seem to have a way of showing up in the house. They get there by different means. One we don't like to acknowledge is their presence in some grains, meal, and other things that we buy for everyday usage. Regardless, they can be a pain in the ….

On occasion I have noticed some of these around my meal worm farms. The spiders may be after them more than my stock. However, I have not had a farm infected with them.

My explanation for this is primarily that the meal worms eat the eggs of any intruders. I do not know if this is true but it is the only explanation that I can offer.

Since these bothersome pests come from grains and nuts and such, they will be drawn to your meal worm farm. I suggest that you do not panic. Still, I do not like them anywhere in the house. There are a number of "moth" traps available that you can use to get rid of the ones flying around. Use whatever works for you, if you have the need. I have had success with products from gardens alive. They have a nice informative catalog and a web site for ordering.

Finally, don't fumigate your meal worm farms. If you have any kind of insect problem wherein you might fumigate your house, remove your farm. This is obvious but you might not think of it.

The next chapter is for those of you who whish to have more meal worms. As long as you take care of them they will breed and produce more meal worms. There are ways to help this process along and increase your herd a couple of times within a year or so.

INCREASING THE HERD

This chapter is for those of you who would like to have more meal worms than your current farm is producing. Once you have the basics of meal worm farming down, increasing your herd is easy. Unless you are making meals of them for yourself, you can surely raise as many as you want.

HOW DO I START ANOTHER FARM?

By this point you probably have a few ideas about doing this. But I hope to give you some helpful information.

The quickest and easiest way to increase your herd is to move them in to a larger container or divide the herd in to two containers when you clean the farm. But you don't have to wait that long and maybe you don't want to.

At any point that you have a farm going, you can start another farm. All you have to do is set up a new container and transfer some of your meal worms, or pupae, or beetles … and maybe eggs.

When I start a new farm, I usually trap some meal worms and move them in to a new container. This is easy and works for me.

Many people prefer to start a new farm by moving beetles. I have also done this and it also works.

Which ever method you use, you should put at least a dozen larvae or beetles in to the new farm. This is to ensure that you will likely have a mix of male and female stock.

As mentioned before, I discourage moving or disturbing the pupae. They are quite delicate. However, I have moved them in the process of setting up another farm. I didn't do it at that time on purpose. I had a container full of both larvae and pupae, and I wanted to harvest some of the meal worms. In harvesting the meal worms I did not want to injure the pupae. So I gently spooned them up and put them in to a new container that I had hastily set up. They, or most of them, morphed in to beetles which did their thing and provided me with more meal worms.

You can also start a farm with eggs. That is, if you can find them, either in your farm or any other way. There is no reason I can think of for pursuing this way of starting a new meal worm farm.

In the previous chapter I mentioned purposefully putting larger pieces of potato in my containers when I have many beetles. One reason is that it seems to me that the beetles require more moisture than the larvae. Another reason is that I believe they lay eggs on or in large pieces of potato that have previously been eaten in to by larvae.

The literature suggests that the eggs are laid in the bedding. I am sure that they are. But I think, and this is my speculation, that eggs are also laid in or on the potato. So, I provide a larger piece of potato when beetles are present for their nourishment and laying of eggs.

One time as an experiment I started a new farm with only a potato from an established farm. I did not know what to expect. Later, I had meal worms. I know this does not prove that there were eggs in or on the potato. There could have been tiny meal worms in the potato. But either way, such is why I hang on to the larger potato pieces that I add when there are beetles. I either start a new farm or leave it there until some time after the beetles have died and any eggs should have hatched.

HOW DO I KEEP MY HERDS HEALTHY?

You already know the most important things to tend to that will keep your meal worms healthy. But there is one more thing to know if you are keeping them for generation after generation, year after year.

Meal worms are living creatures. You know how to provide them with a healthy environment, food, and shelter. In order to produce healthy future generations they also need a healthy gene pool.

In my experience, depending on the conditions, meal worms will reproduce 2 to 3 times a year. That can vary a lot as you have already read.

Regardless, after a number of years you have stock that is becoming inbred. As with all breeding creatures this tends over time to produce offspring that are increasingly prone to be less healthy.

At one point in time it seemed to me that my meal worms were getting smaller and less prolific with each generation. Since I had a basic understanding of the gene pool concept, I added new stock to my existing stock. That is about the only thing I can suggest to do to keep your gene pool healthy. I have no other evidence for this than my experience but I think that adding some other new meal worms every two to three years serves this purpose.

This isn't a big deal if you go fishing a lot. If I forget my meal worms or run out and I can buy some at a bait shop I do so and whatever is left I add to the farm. Otherwise you might have to buy a dozen in 2 or 3 years to keep your gene pool healthy.

Follow these guidelines and you should have plenty of healthy meal worms for your purposes. But, you may run in to the problem of having too many.

WHAT IF I HAVE TOO MANY?

What if you have too many and it is not because they are over crowded? As in, having more than you need or know what to do with? It can happen.

The first thing I'd say is that you have been successful. The second might be that you didn't believe me.

Like if they are over crowded, you could take some fishing. Or, you could buy another copy of this book and give it with meal worms to a friend!

Unfortunately, the idea of this guide is to help you raise them and have as many as you want. However, I have a couple of suggestions for you if you really have too many.

You can put some on ice. When you bought your initial stock somebody probably took them out of a refrigerator. They are kept that way not just to keep them fresh. The lower temperature delays the larvae from morphing in to beetles. The little creatures will become dormant at low temperatures for three months or more. Just put some in a container similar to the one you bought initially and put them away. This way you will have some on hand to pull out for fishing or feeding your pet at any time for the next couple of months.

As an aside, I believe that the refrigeration contributes to different morphing times. If you have meal worms in your farm that morph at different times of the year, it may depend on when you bought them and added them to the farm.

You can purposefully, depending on where you live, put some out in a small container for the birds or other creatures. Or eat them yourself.

If you really have a lot, you might offer to exchange them for something at your local fish or pet store. I used to exchange fish for fish food. Or you might post a note saying that you have meal worms for sale, exchange, or the taking.

Other than these suggestions, you might harvest some and put them out in your yard in a small container than will hold them as bird food. The next chapter discusses how to use them in feeding your pets.

FEEDING PETS MEAL WORMS

When I had my chameleon I mostly fed it lettuce and meal worms. I think it may have also eaten earthworms and small bits of raw hamburger. As mentioned elsewhere, there are many creatures that are kept as pets that like meal worms as part of their diet. In my youth I also fed meal worms to a turtle and a horned toad. The meal worm is a good food source that is rich with protein and well liked by many creatures.

This is a short chapter because I have not had any of the other animals as pets that are said to like meal worms as part of their diets. I do know that even among those pets that eat meal worms, there are differences in the extent to which meal worms should constitute part of their diet. For instance, young iguanas are more carnivorous than adults and require more protein in their diets. As they mature, they become mostly vegetarian and any meal worms should be occasional supplements if any are fed at all.

The best thing you can do is to learn about whatever pet you have. If you purchase one from a pet store, you should ask the representatives about the care and feeding of your pet. They will also likely have free literature or books for purchase to help you learn about your pet. You can probably find books or get books through your library. And, of course, you can surf the web for information on your pet.

FISHING WITH MEAL WORMS

If you are raising meal worms for fishing bait, you probably already know what a great bait they make. If not, you are in for a real treat.

WHAT KIND OF FISH CAN I CATCH?

You can catch almost any fresh water fish with meal worms. Where I live, I've caught most every kind of fish that swims in the waters where I wet a line. I use them primarily to catch bluegill (brim or bream), warmouth (or rock bass), red ear, catfish, bass (large or small mouth and stripped), some times crappie, and in the few places around here stocked with them, trout. I have also caught carp, buffalo, drum, perch, and sheep's head (depending on what you call these fish where you live). I have even pulled in a turtle and a snake while using meal worms.

When I go fishing I like to throw lures. I often have limited success. I like to blame that on fishing heavily pressured public waters; however, I just might not be that good of a fisherman. Regardless, if I am having a slow day and want to have some fun, I pull out my secret weapon – the meal worm. This is especially true if I am camping and want to put some fish in the pan, on the grill, or over the fire. Even I can almost always catch enough of something to make a meal of when I'm using my meal worms.

I don't want to insult your fishing skills, but I have a couple of tips for fishing with meal worms that might be helpful if you are new to using meal worms as bait. These follow the next section which has to do with harvesting and transporting your meal worms for a fishing trip. There are certain considerations worth paying attention to if you want to get your meal worms to the fishing hole and be able to use them while there.

HOW DO I TRANSPORT MY MEAL WORMS?

Before you do anything else, you need something to put them in. Do not put them in a cardboard container. This may seem obvious, but I blew it once. Yes, they will eat through it.

You can use a container like the kind in which you obtained your initial stock. I prefer other kinds of containers to transport my meal worms. The typical thinner plastic containers with snap on type lids are easily bent or crushed. If the container is bent it is difficult to replace the lid so that it seals well and then it is particularly easy to be knocked off or pop off.

My preference is a hard plastic container with a screw on lid like what a small amount of instant coffee might come in. The plastic doesn't break or crack easily. By screwing on, the lid is secure. You can see the contents. And, if you should drop of knock it in to the water it will float long enough to be retrieved.

The next best thing in my opinion is a plastic tropical fish food container, say 4 to 10 ounce size. Whatever kind of container you use, make sure to put a couple of small holes in the lid to provide fresh air for the meal worms.

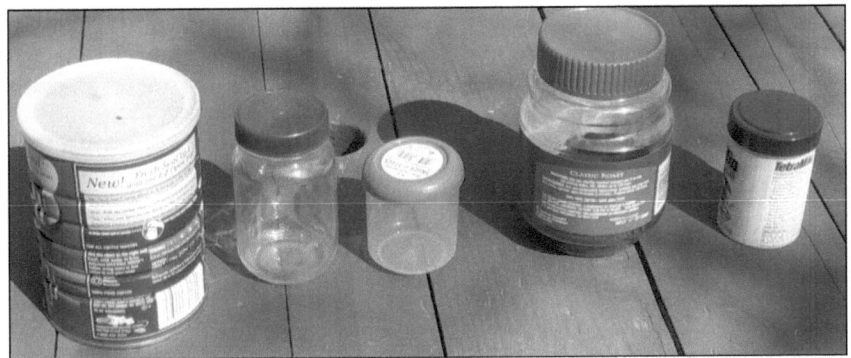

The size of the container you use to transport your meal worms will depend mostly on how many you plan to take with you. If you are going on an extended trip of several days to a week or more, I suggest taking one large container and a smaller one. Transport your meal worms to your camp or home base in the larger container. Then put however many you want to take with you for a morning or evening outing in to the smaller container.

When transporting your meal worms you should treat them as much as possible as if they were at home. They are going to be crowded, jostled, and subjected to more extreme conditions. Give them adequate bedding. I like to add some fresh corn meal and even a tiny bit of potato or carrot.

The most important thing to do with your meal worms when you're taking them fishing is to maintain their environment. It is usually warm or fairly hot when I take meal worms fishing. They travel well in a cooler, though I wouldn't put them directly on ice.

A small sandwich or six-pack container also works well, adding a sealable bag with a couple of ice cubes or a small plastic bottle of frozen water. Keeping the ice in a sealed storage or freezer bag or in a plastic bottle prevents accidentally drowning your meal worms.

If by chance you are out when it is likely to freeze, take the meal worms in to your tent or lodging with you or leave them in your vehicle. When you are actually using the meal worms, keep the container out of direct sun light so they won't get over heated.

HOW DO I HARVEST MEAL WORMS FOR BAIT?

The easiest thing to do is to put some food in a corner of the farm the night before you plan to go fishing. In the morning just scoop up a handful, bedding and all, and place it in your transportation container. The success of this method will depend on how many meal worms are on the farm and how many you are hoping to harvest for your trip.

You many also use the paper plate technique, starting a day or two ahead of time to make sure you have the number of meal worms desired. Another method is to place a small piece of screen over part of the surface of the farm with some fresh potato or carrot.

Then, some time later, lift the screen out, allowing much of the bedding and small meal worms to fall back in to the farm. If you have a low supply of meal worms at the time, you can also take scoops of bedding and sift it through the screen to harvest some for bait.

If you have many pupae, you should gently move them out of the harvesting area. Similarly, you will want to gently put any beetles that are harvested back on the farm.

There are exceptions to the above. If you have too many meal worms, if most of the herd are pupae or beetles, or if you just want to try it, you can also use the pupae and beetles as bait.

I don't generally recommend this for reasons mentioned elsewhere, but I have done it before. Both will work well as bait. They are both quite fragile though, especially the pupae. I will just say that it is tricky business using them as bait. Besides, if I am short of meal worms for any reason, I use it as an opportunity to buy some and use any left over as new additions to my stock.

HOW DO I USE MEAL WORMS AS BAIT?

There are many ways to use your meal worms to catch fish. How you use them will depend mostly on where you're fishing, how you want to fish, and what you want to catch. I have used them in all of the following ways:

- with a small bobber and no weight in shallower water;
- with a bobber (or slip bobber) and weight in deeper water;
- bottom fishing;
- jigging (with no weight, small weight, or with a jig head);
- tipping a spinner or as replacement for the artificial bait; and,
- as a live "fly" with a fly rod.

Whatever way you use the meal worm as bait, you have to put it on the hook. You will have to find your preferred way to do this.

For the most part, I fish with one or two meal worms. I recommend using a hook that isn't much larger than the meal worms. A number 6 or slightly smaller hook works for me.

On occasion, particularly if bottom fishing for catfish or such, I will use 2 to 4 meal worms at a time. At those times I use a larger hook.

The main thing about putting them on the hook and keeping them there is to make use of the exoskeleton. The segmented exoskeleton starts behind the head. As the meal worm naturally tends to curve in on its belly side, which sort of follows the curvature of a hook, I suggest hooking them from that side. This means starting the hook in just after the head and bringing it out close to the end of the body. Do this so that just enough of the hook is exposed to catch your fish.

The fairly docile meal worm can become quite active when picked up and handled. If you are holding it so the top side is facing you, you can do the same thing from that position. Generally you want to hook your meal worm in these ways. There are exceptions, but most of the time if you hook them in other ways, they will be easily torn from the hook and you will be doing more feeding of the fish than catching them.

ANY OTHER TIPS?

I have just two other tips to share. The first has to do with the nature of the meal worm. The other I offer by way of a fishing story.

As live bait, the meal worm isn't very lively. Yet, that doesn't hinder its effectiveness. It is, after all, real food and fresh. It is my belief that it has an odor which rings the dinner bell for fish. It seems to me that this is strengthened when the meal worm has been injured, as in partly stripped from the hook by some would be stringer occupant or tiny thief. For this reason and to make the most use of your meal worms, I recommend leaving any small pieces that are left on your hook if it has been stripped and adding a new meal worm to what is there.

The way I most like to fish the meal worm, especially for pan fish, is with a small bobber and no weight. I prefer the small pencil bobbers. When using light tackle, the thin bobber goes through the air while providing enough weight to make decent casts. The lack of any weight allows the meal worm to slowly fall giving subtle but noticeable action to the bait. Also, slight movements of the rod will pull the meal worm towards the surface allowing it to slowly fall again. In my experience, if I am in the right spot, at least half of the fish I catch hit the bait within seconds after the cast.

This works well in shallow water that is two to four feet deep. If you are fishing deeper water or have windy conditions you would probably want to add a little weight. I would suggest a small split shot that is as far up on the line as is appropriate for the conditions. If you have a little wind you can let the wind move the bait for you.

Although meal worms, of some kind, are native to most of the continental United States, I think that fish have limited access to them -- except as bait. This tends to make the meal worm a special treat. There is at least one way that fish have access to insects like meal worms. Please indulge my telling of the following fishing story and you will see what I mean.

On a late fall day many years ago my son and I went camping. After setting up camp we went fishing. We threw some lures and even dropped some red worms in the water to no avail. Even though the wind was getting stronger we brought out the meal worms. We still had little success until we hit the right spot.

Then we started catching bluegills that were 7 to 9 inches and larger, one after the other. The local site specific regulations imposed a limit of 25 per day. We not only had to start keeping count but as we approached the limit we started returning the smaller ones.

In a little over an hour (really) we both had our limits. More importantly, we had a great time. How did that happen?

I wasn't sure myself, at first. But I realized we were fishing under a large nut tree and the wind was blowing the nuts in to the water. A check of the nuts that didn't make it in to the water revealed that they were infested with the larval form of some insect that was similar to a meal worm. When the nuts fell in to the water, the worms would seek to escape and this created a feeding frenzy among the fish.

If you find such a place with similar conditions and you are not practicing catch and release, you will have many fish to clean!

You've heard it said that a bad day of fishing is better than a good day at work. It's never a bad day of fishing when you're in good company: the company of a good friend, and your meal worms!

BIBLIOGRAPHY

American Heritage Dictionary of the English Language, Fourth Edition, Mealworm.

Arnett, Ross H. & Thomas, Michael C., <u>American Beetles</u>, vol I (2000).

ASU-Ask A Biologist: 11/23/04.
http://askabiologist.asu.edu/research/beetles/lifecycle.html

Collier's Encyclopedia. 1991 Mac Millan Educational Company, NY, NY.

Crowsan, Roy A., <u>Biology of the Coleoptera</u>. (1981)

Evans, Arthur V. & Bellany, Charles L., <u>An Inordinate Fondness for Beetles</u>. (1975)

Harris, C. Jack. <u>A STEP-BY-STEP BOOK ABOUT IGUANAS</u>. New Jersey: T.F.H. Publications, Inc., 1990.

Himmelman, John. <u>A MEALWORM'S LIFE</u>. (New York: Children's Press, Inc. 2001)

Mealworm. http://en.wikipedia.org/wiki/Tenebrio_molitor

Mealworm. Academic American Encyclopedia. Grollier Inc. Danbury, Connecticut, 1994.

Meal Worms. http://www.msu.edu/~ragsdale/mealworm.htm

MealWorms. Meal Worms at <wormman.com>. 11/23/04.

Pielou, D. P. and Gunn, D. L. The Humidity Behaviour of the Mealworm Beetle, *Tenebrio Molitor* L: I. The Reaction to Differences of Humidity. *Journal of Experimental Biology* 17,286-294 (1940) [online abstract]

Rueda, L. M. and Axtell, R. C. Temperature-dependent development and survival of the lesser mealworm, Alphitobius diaperinus. Department of Entomology, North Carolina University, Raleigh, USA. [online abstract]

Renault D.: Salin C.; Vannier G.; Veronon, P. Journal of Thermal Biology. v24, Number 4, August 1999, pp. 229-236.

Salin, C., Vernon, P. and Vannier G. The supercooling and high temperature stupor points of the adult lesser mealworm *Alphitobius diaperinus* (Coleoptera: Tenebrionidae). [online abstract]

Salin, C., Vernon P. and Vannier, G. Effects of temperature and humidity in adults of the lesser mealworm, Alphitobius diaperinus (Coleoptera: Tenebrionidae) J Insect Physio. 1999 Oct; 45 (10):907-914. [online abstract]

Schaffer, Donna. <u>Mealworms</u>. 1999 MacMillan Educational Company, NY, NY.

teachersnetwork.org. Darkling Beetle/Meal Worm. 11/23/2004. http://www.teachersnetwork.rog/dcs/critter/mealworm/

White, Richard E.; "beetle". Grolier Multimedia Encycolpedia. Scholastic Library Publishing. 2005 <http://gme.Grolier.com> (March 1, 2005)

NOTES

www.ingramcontent.com/pod-product-compliance
Ingram Content Group UK Ltd.
Pitfield, Milton Keynes, MK11 3LW, UK
UKHW041959230426
12048UKWH00008B/413